REPRODUCTION TO BIRTH

Design	David West
	Children's Book Design
Editorial Planning	Clark Robinson Limited
Picture Researcher	Emma Krikler
Illustrators	Aziz Khan
	Peter Harper
Consultant	Dr. Stuart Milligan
	Physiologist

© Aladdin Books 1991

First published in
the United States in 1991 by
Gloucester Press
387 Park Avenue South
New York, NY 10016

Printed in Belgium

Library of Congress Cataloging-in-Publication Data

Twist, Clint.
    Reproduction to birth : projects with biology / Clint Twist.
        p.   cm. -- (Hands on science)
    Includes index.
    Summary: Covers the different methods of reproduction of various
species, genetics, heredity, and the implications of genetic
engineering, including appropriate hands on projects.
    ISBN 0-531-17294-5
    1. Reproduction--Juvenile literature. [1. Reproduction.
2. Reproduction--Experiments. 3. Experiments.] I. Title.
II. Series.
QP251.5.T85   1991
591.16--dc20   91-6818   CIP   AC

941.983

HANDS · ON · SCIENCE

REPRODUCTION TO BIRTH

Clint Twist

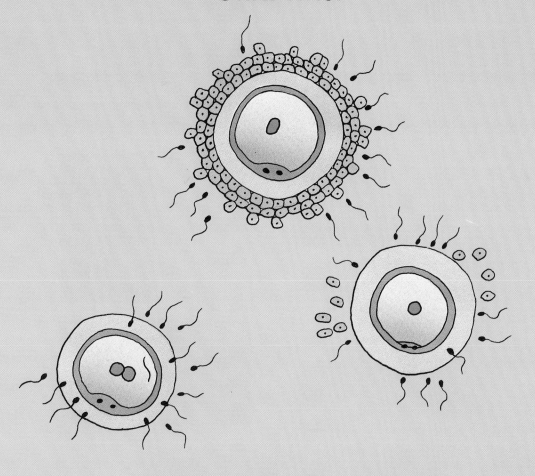

GLOUCESTER PRESS
New York · London · Toronto · Sydney

CONTENTS

This book is about reproduction in animals — from courtship behavior and mating to birth. The book tells you about eggs and how they are fertilized. It also describes how eggs develop into young animals. There are "hands on" projects for you to try, which you can do in a park or yard, or using everyday items as equipment. And there are "did you know?" panels of information for fun.

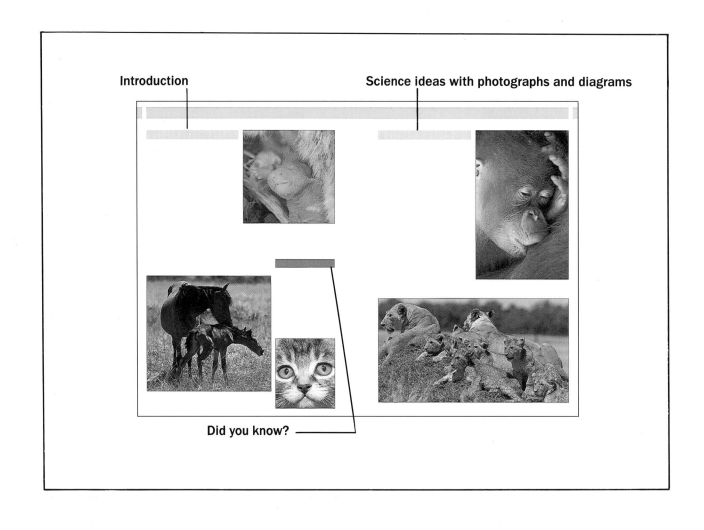

Introduction

Science ideas with photographs and diagrams

Did you know?

INTRODUCTION

Reproduction is the creation of new individuals from existing members of the population. It is a characteristic of all living species. The members of a species must reproduce if the species as a whole is going to survive. An essential part of this is information on how to develop passing from parents to their offspring. This information is stored in a substance called DNA.

Many tiny single-celled animals reproduce asexually. In asexual reproduction, the creation of a new individual requires only a single parent. Offspring created by asexual reproduction are identical copies of their parent.

Larger animals almost always reproduce sexually. New individuals are created by two parents, one female and one male. The basis of sexual reproduction is the female egg, which needs to be fertilized by a male sperm. The fertilized egg then develops into a new animal.

Frogs lay large numbers of eggs.

Many of the smaller organisms reproduce asexually. In asexual reproduction, only one parent is necessary in order to produce offspring. One advantage of this is that a large population can be created by just one individual. Some animals only reproduce asexually in conditions when rapid reproduction is useful.

BINARY FISSION

The most basic method of reproduction is binary fission. This is a method of asexual reproduction in which an organism duplicates itself by simply splitting into two. Binary fission happens almost entirely in microscopic organisms that consist of just a single cell, such as amoebas.

After binary fission, each new organism is only half the size of the "parent" organism. When feeding has increased their size, the new organisms can also undergo binary fission. This would produce a total of four organisms. These new organisms in turn can divide. The population can continue to double in size in this way until something stops the increase in numbers, such as the food supply running out.

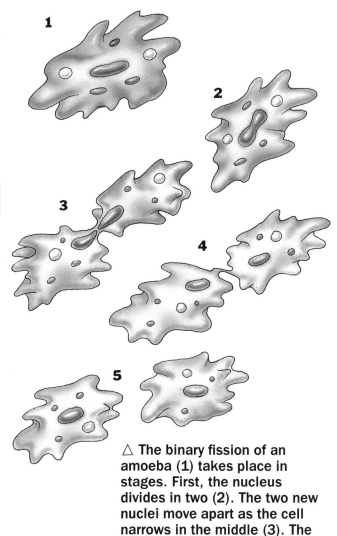

△ The binary fission of an amoeba (1) takes place in stages. First, the nucleus divides in two (2). The two new nuclei move apart as the cell narrows in the middle (3). The narrowing continues (4) until the cell splits into two (5).

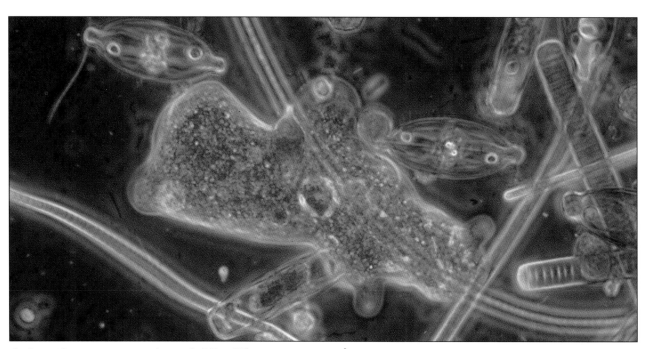

△ Amoebas measure about 0.25 millimeters.

REGENERATION

Larger animals that have simple structures can also reproduce by binary fission. Sea anemones, for example, can divide vertically down the center. The process is much more complicated than in amoebas, because anemones are many-celled animals. After dividing, the two halves of the anemone each grow a new replacement half by a process known as regeneration.

If an anemone is torn from a rock, any portion remaining on the rock can regenerate into a complete individual. Other nonmobile animals, such as sponges and corals, also have the ability to grow a new individual from small pieces that have broken off.

Flatworms are more complex animals. They have brains, eyespots and many internal organs. But they have great powers of regeneration. When cut into pieces, each piece grows into a complete new flatworm. Some species of flatworm can reproduce by deliberately dividing themselves across the middle. This is a quick way of producing new individuals.

Starfish often regrow a missing arm. Sometimes, a detached arm may regenerate the rest of the starfish.

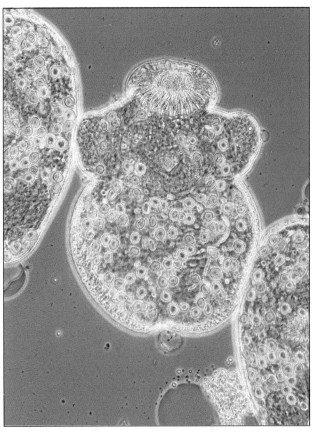

△ Tapeworm larvae can grow many new segments by a process of regeneration.

▽ Planarian flatworms have distinct heads and tails. But if a flatworm is cut into three pieces, even the tail piece will regenerate back into a complete animal.

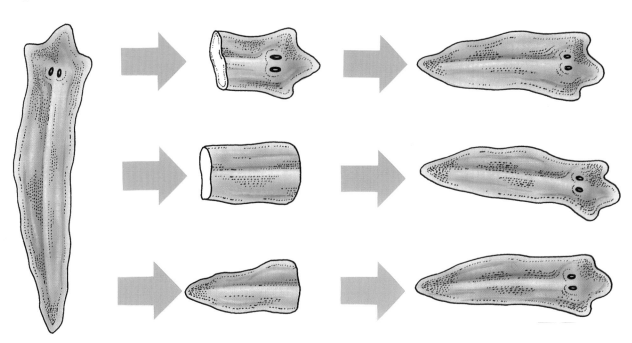

7

BUDDING

Some organisms reproduce asexually by budding. An example of such an animal is the hydra, which can grow a new individual from a bud on the side of its body. At first, the bud is just a small swelling. It grows into a miniature version of the adult before it breaks off from the parent. Animals that are produced by budding are often referred to as "daughters" of the parent animal.

Sea anemones are closely related to hydras, and can also reproduce by budding. In many species, the buds grow inside the body cavity of the adult. When they have grown large enough to survive on their own, the daughters are ejected through the adult anemone's mouth. They then anchor themselves to rocks.

Some segmented worms can reproduce by a form of budding. The new individual forms from the lower half of the worm, and the two halves then separate.

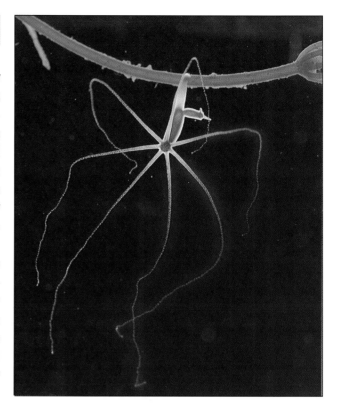

△ Hydras develop buds when food is plentiful. If food is scarce, the parent may absorb the bud back into its body.

INSECTS' EGGS

You can find insects' eggs in many places. The eggs are always very small — usually less than a millimeter across. The easiest place to find insects' eggs is stuck to the bottom of leaves. These are often the eggs of butterflies.

Make notes of all the eggs you can find: how big they are and what color, where you found them and how many there are. See if you can find out what kind of insect laid them. Never take away the eggs: they may belong to a rare species.

As well as insects' eggs, you can also find spiders' eggs quite easily. Many spiders lay their eggs in their webs. The eggs are wrapped in a little package of the silk that the web is made from.

Make a chart for notes

Spiders' eggs

Insects' eggs

PARTHENOGENESIS

A special form of asexual reproduction called parthenogenesis is found in some more complex types of animal, and especially among insects. Parthenogenesis is the process by which females by themselves produce eggs that develop into new animals. In many ways, parthenogenesis is like sexual reproduction, but it occurs without the need of sperm from the male to fertilize the eggs. Usually, all the eggs develop into female animals. This means that a whole generation of animals may be produced that consists entirely of one sex.

Aphids reproduce by parthenogenesis as part of an annual cycle. In spring, female insects are born that lay eggs without mating. The eggs soon hatch into more females, and during the summer there are several entirely female generations. At the beginning of fall, the females lay some eggs that hatch into males. When they have hatched, mating takes place. The eggs that are laid after mating remain dormant during the winter, and then hatch into females at the beginning of spring.

Daphnia, the water flea, is not in fact an insect, but a crustacean — a relative of such animals as shrimps. Daphnia, which lives in freshwater ponds, often reproduces by parthenogenesis. In some species, the females can produce two sorts of eggs: ones that develop by themselves, and ones that need to be fertilized by sperm.

△ It is possible to see the eggs being held inside the transparent body covering of a female daphnia. The eggs are usually released. But sometimes they are kept inside the body until the animal dies.

◁ Aphids damage plants by feeding on their sap. A single female aphid can quickly produce a population of many thousands. This is why gardeners and farmers consider aphids to be such a serious pest.

Sexual reproduction takes place by the joining of female and male sex cells after mating. The big advantage of sexual reproduction is that new animals are formed from material provided by two parents. This is important for several reasons, such as good characteristics being spread through the species.

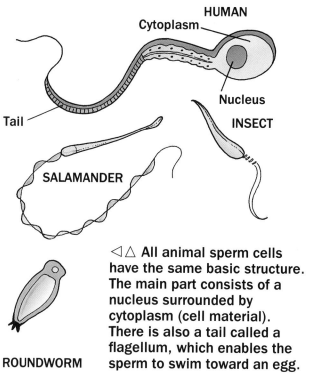

HUMAN

Cytoplasm

Nucleus

Tail

INSECT

SALAMANDER

◁△ All animal sperm cells have the same basic structure. The main part consists of a nucleus surrounded by cytoplasm (cell material). There is also a tail called a flagellum, which enables the sperm to swim toward an egg.

ROUNDWORM

EGG AND SPERM

All animals produce special sex cells, which are known as gametes. Female gametes are called eggs, and male gametes are called sperm. These cells are produced by special sex organs: the ovary in females, and the testis in males. Eggs are usually much larger than sperm because they store material needed for when they grow; they are also produced in smaller numbers.

Neither gamete can develop into a new animal by itself (parthenogenesis is a rare exception). A new animal can grow only after fertilization. During fertilization, a sperm breaks through the membrane that surrounds an egg. The nucleus of the sperm then joins with the nucleus of the egg. This creates a cell known as a fertilized egg, or zygote.

The most important feature of sexual reproduction is the fusion (joining) of the nuclei. The nucleus of each gamete contains half of the information needed to make a new individual. In order to understand the process, it is necessary to look more closely at how cells divide.

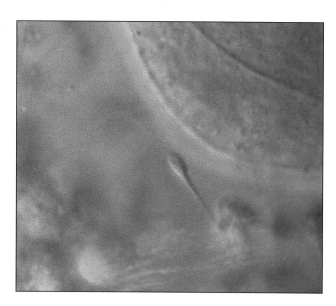

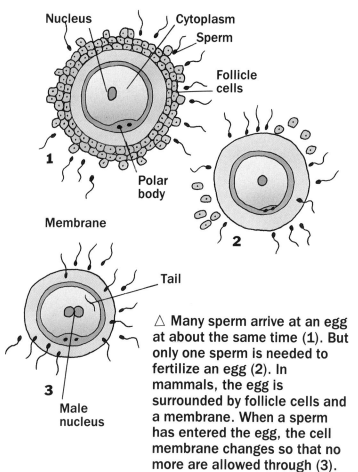

Nucleus

Cytoplasm

Sperm

Follicle cells

Membrane

1

Polar body

2

Tail

Male nucleus

3

△ Many sperm arrive at an egg at about the same time (1). But only one sperm is needed to fertilize an egg (2). In mammals, the egg is surrounded by follicle cells and a membrane. When a sperm has entered the egg, the cell membrane changes so that no more are allowed through (3).

CELL DIVISION

Cells reproduce themselves by dividing into two new cells. This most commonly occurs when an animal is growing. Each new cell must contain all the information it needs about how it will develop and how it will work. This information is stored in the nucleus of the cell by a substance called DNA (which stands for deoxyribonucleic acid).

The DNA is divided into chromosomes. These only become visible when a cell is about to divide. Different animals have different numbers of chromosomes – for example, humans have 46. A cell that has a full set of chromosomes is known as a diploid cell. The chromosomes of a cell are in pairs. Each one of a pair has information about the same things. The diagrams here show what happens to only one pair of chromosomes.

Normal cell division is known as mitosis. Each chromosome is duplicated, producing two chromatids, which are joined in the middle. The chromatids from each chromosome move to opposite ends of the cell. Then the cell divides in the middle. The chromatids become chromosomes, so each new cell has a pair. The two new cells are just like the old cell, and both are diploid.

When producing gametes, cell division is called meiosis. Chromatids form and the cell divides. But the chromatids of each chromosome stay together, and the cell splits between the chromosomes. This gives two cells with only half the number of chromosomes. These are haploid cells. The new cells divide, splitting the chromatids. In the end there are four gametes, each with one chromosome (each gamete is haploid).

In fertilization, two gametes join together to produce a zygote. The zygote is a diploid cell. This cell will then divide by mitosis. You can now see that in a diploid cell, each chromosome in a pair comes from a different parent.

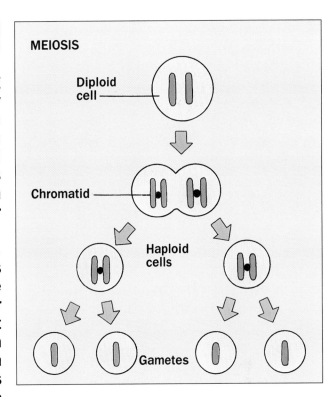

MEIOSIS

Diploid cell

Chromatid

Haploid cells

Gametes

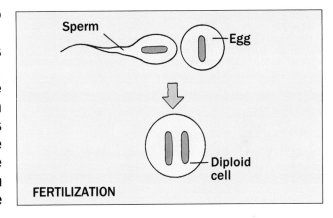

Sperm

Egg

Diploid cell

FERTILIZATION

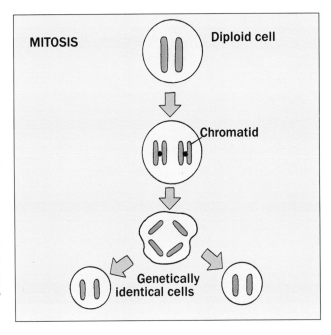

MITOSIS

Diploid cell

Chromatid

Genetically identical cells

With most animals that live in water — for example, fish and amphibians — fertilization takes place outside the body. This process is known as external fertilization. Both sexes release gametes (eggs and sperm) into the water, and the sperm swim around until they make contact with the floating eggs.

COURTSHIP

Before external fertilization, courtship usually takes place. There are two basic purposes of courtship. First, it helps animals to know that they are opposite sexes of the same species. Second, it allows each animal to know that the other is sexually mature and ready to reproduce. Sexual reproduction can only take place if both parents produce and release gametes at the same time.

Courtship takes many different forms. For example, most species of frog give distinctive cries to show that they are ready to mate; many fish go through a series of special moves, like a sort of dance. There may also be signals from physical changes, such as the color of the animal's skin changing.

NEST BUILDING

Nest building is quite unusual among fish and other animals that live in water. Usually their eggs float freely or are attached to a surface. Some fish do build nests, however, and this is often closely linked with courtship.

Female trout and salmon make shallow scrapes in gravel at the bottom of streams. This attracts males, and means that when the female lays her eggs there is a male nearby to fertilize them. With sticklebacks, it is the male that builds a nest. This attracts females, who lay eggs which the male can fertilize.

△ The stickleback is one of the few fish that builds a nest.

△ The color of these male toads attracts females.

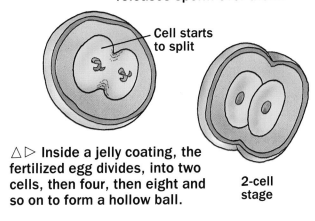

△ When a female jewel fish has laid her eggs, a male releases sperm over them.

RELEASE OF EGGS AND SPERM

In fish and amphibians, the process of laying eggs and fertilization is known as spawning. Some species of fish spawn in shoals (groups), with a large number of individuals releasing clouds of eggs and sperm at the same time. It is just a matter of chance whether a particular egg is fertilized by a particular sperm. Other fish species form definite female-male pairs, which spawn separately.

Among amphibians, such as frogs, forming pairs is the most common method of spawning. Two adults remain in physical contact through the whole process. Being in close contact gives the best chance of eggs and sperm meeting when they are released.

Cell starts to split

△▷ Inside a jelly coating, the fertilized egg divides, into two cells, then four, then eight and so on to form a hollow ball.

2-cell stage

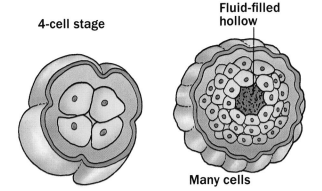

4-cell stage

Fluid-filled hollow

Many cells

EARLY DEVELOPMENT

Once an egg has been fertilized and becomes a zygote, it begins to develop into a new animal. The zygote grows by dividing into two cells, which themselves then divide and so on (this is a process of mitosis). Each time the cells divide, the number of cells doubles.

During the first stages of the process, the cells multiply evenly until they form a hollow sphere, which is known as a blastocyst. By this stage, the new in-dividual is known as an embryo. The embryo then starts to develop differently. Instead of all the new cells being the same as each other, special cells now start to appear. Each type of cell

develops into a different part of the new animal's body.

As development continues, the embryo takes on a definite shape, and internal organs start to form. During the very early stages of development, all animal embryos have a similar appearance. The visible characteristics of different animals only appear later on.

Fish and amphibian eggs often have a jellylike coating. Inside this protective layer, the fertilized egg develops very rapidly. In some frog species, it takes just six hours for the zygote to become a blastocyst containing some 10,000 cells. About 48 hours later, frog embryos have already taken on a distinctive tadpole shape that is clearly visible through the jelly coating.

CARE OF EGGS

In the open sea, fish eggs usually drift in the water. In coastal and fresh waters, the eggs often have a sticky surface which holds them together in clusters or long tapes. These eggs can become attached to a stone or plant.

The only thing an embryo needs from outside an egg is oxygen. In very sheltered water — such as a nest — the amount of oxygen in the water may become quite low. The embryos may then suffocate. Male sticklebacks solve this problem by fanning their fins to sweep fresh water over the eggs.

Only a few other fish, such as the freshwater bass, guard their eggs. A larger number of amphibians take care of their eggs. The most unusual example is the gastric brooding frog of Australia. After fertilization, the female swallows the eggs and they develop and hatch inside her stomach.

△ It is possible to see the developing embryos inside translucent carp eggs. The eyes are clearly visible. You can also make out the tails that the larvae will swim with.

△ The larvae of dogfish can be seen developing in their egg cases, known as mermaid's purses. Here, one has already hatched.

HATCHING

Fish and amphibians lay very large numbers of eggs. For example, large toads can lay more than 20,000 eggs. This is mainly because a great many of these eggs will be eaten by predators.

Inside each egg, the developing embryo is nourished by yolk until it becomes a larva. When it is ready to hatch, the larva produces chemicals that start to dissolve the jelly coating around the egg. It then starts to make swimming movements, which help to free it from the jelly.

Fish eggs usually hatch quite quickly. Eggs in warm water tend to hatch more quickly than those in cold water. The eggs of a few tropical fish hatch in less than 24 hours. Most eggs hatch in two or three weeks. In a few cold-water species, the eggs do not hatch for about four months. Frog and toad eggs usually hatch in under two weeks.

▽ Tadpoles breathe with gills. After a while, the gills disappear and they breathe through spiracles. Finally they start to breathe through their mouths into lungs.

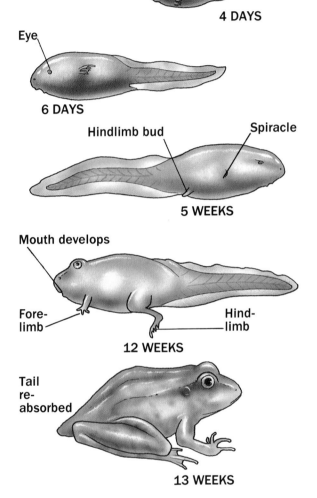

External gills

4 DAYS

Eye

6 DAYS

Hindlimb bud

Spiracle

5 WEEKS

Mouth develops

Fore-limb

Hind-limb

12 WEEKS

Tail re-absorbed

13 WEEKS

CARE OF YOUNG

The care of eggs and young offspring by the parents is known as brooding. The larvae of fish and amphibians are still in great danger of being eaten after they have hatched. This is another reason why fish and amphibians lay so many eggs — to make sure that at least some of them survive. With fish, looking after larvae is even more unusual than taking care of eggs. A few fish do guard their young. Examples are freshwater bass, some sticklebacks and Siamese fighting fish.

An interesting example of brooding is the several species of mouthbreeder fish. The fertilized eggs hatch and the larvae continue to develop entirely within a parent's mouth.

Care of larvae is more common in amphibians. This is especially true of those whose adults spend most of their time out of water. Examples are salamanders and tree frogs.

△ The male arrow-poison frog from South America lives on land and carries first eggs and then tadpoles on its back.

Fish larvae grow directly into adult fish. Amphibian larvae, however, undergo a complete body change, known as metamorphosis. Frog and toad larvae are called tadpoles. Their development takes place gradually over a period of a few weeks.

Some insects also go through metamorphosis. For example, butterfly eggs hatch into caterpillars, which grow but do not change in shape. They then become pupas (cover themselves in hard cases) before emerging as butterflies.

Reptiles and birds reproduce by internal fertilization. Their eggs are fertilized while they are still inside the female's body. The female lays the eggs after fertilization. The embryo develops inside the egg, which has a protective shell. Young reptiles and birds hatch out as miniature versions of the adult.

COURTSHIP

Reptiles and birds form mating pairs. Sometimes the pair will split up as soon as they have mated. But often they stay together for the breeding season.

Male birds often establish their own territories. Their calls are both to attract females and to challenge other males. In the presence of females, the males of many species give complex displays of movement and color.

Courtship is not so complex among reptiles. It is seen most in lizards. Like birds, the males of some lizard species are more brightly colored during the breeding season.

△ Male peacocks display their brightly colored tail feathers as part of courtship rituals.

BIRD COURTSHIP

You can quite often see birds courting. Courting usually, but not always, happens in the spring. You can often tell the male and female birds apart because they are different sizes or colors. You may see dancing or strutting, nods of the head, beaks being tapped together and many other sorts of behavior. Make notes of everything you see.

FERTILIZATION

Reptiles and birds have only a single opening (or vent) in the lower part of their bodies. This vent leads to a cavity known as the cloaca, which is used both for excretion and during reproduction.

In birds, sperm produced by the testes pass down a tube to the male cloaca. During mating, the male presses his vent against that of the female, and sperm is transferred from one cloaca to the other. From the female cloaca, the sperm swim up a passageway toward the eggs, which are released from the ovaries. The sperm fertilize the eggs.

The eggs of reptiles and birds need to be fairly large, because miniature adults hatch from them. Birds and reptiles produce many fewer eggs than amphibians and fishes do.

NESTS AND EGGS

Among birds, nest building is sometimes linked to courtship. An example is the African weaverbird. The male weaverbird makes the framework of the nest to attract a mate. With most birds, nest building is done by the female, although the male bird sometimes helps.

Birds' nests are often quite elaborate and take a lot of effort to build. They have to be a safe place for eggs, and also be a nursery for young birds.

The nests made by reptiles are much simpler. They are built by the female just before she lays her eggs. Some reptiles, such as the Florida alligator, heap mud over their eggs. Others, such as turtles, bury their eggs in sand.

▷ An African weaverbird's nest is built by the male. It weaves the nest mostly from grass in a tree where it is fairly safe from predators.

△ Mating black rat snakes twine around each other.

Eggs are produced in an organ called the ovary. They then pass down a tube (the oviduct), in birds to the cloaca. Eggs are usually fertilized just outside the ovary at the top of the oviduct. As an egg travels down the oviduct, it grows its tough outer shell. This creates a sealed environment that stops the embryo from drying out. The eggs of reptiles have a flexible leathery shell. Birds' eggs have a hard, brittle shell. Both types of shell have tiny holes that allow oxygen to pass inside and reach the embryo.

The eggs that are laid by a female at one time are known as a clutch. The number of eggs in the clutch is usually about the same in any particular species of reptile or bird. Reptiles most commonly lay larger clutches than do birds. A crocodile clutch may contain 70 eggs, and that of a turtle 200. Among birds, quails lay the biggest clutches with about 20 eggs. Clutches of five eggs or less are much more common.

INCUBATION

Birds are warm-blooded animals — they can keep themselves warm, even if their environment is cold. Bird's eggs must be kept warm if the embryo is going to continue developing after leaving a bird's body. Keeping eggs warm until they hatch is known as incubation. Birds incubate their eggs by sitting on them. Warmth is transferred to the eggs from an area on the bird's underside known as the brood patch. A layer of insulation that lines the inside of the nest, such as feathers and dry grass, helps to prevent heat from escaping. In most species, both sexes incubate the eggs.

Reptiles are cold-blooded — they obtain body heat from their environment. The warmth of the surrounding air or earth is usually enough to incubate reptile eggs. It is unusual for reptile parents to incubate their eggs.

△ A few species of snake incubate their eggs. For example, some female pythons warm themselves in the sun and then coil around their eggs to transfer the heat.

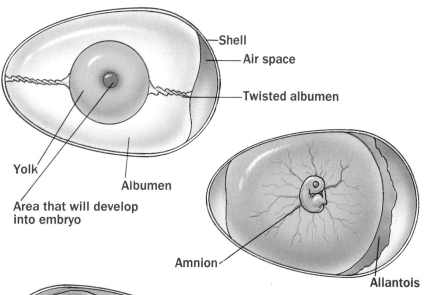

Shell
Air space
Twisted albumen
Yolk
Albumen
Area that will develop into embryo
Amnion
Allantois

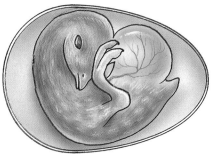

△ As it develops, a bird embryo feeds first off the albumen and then off the yolk. The embryo is surrounded by a membrane called the amnion. Another membrane, the allantois, forms a pocket for waste products. The air space gets bigger as water evaporates through the shell.

DID YOU KNOW?

The sex of some reptiles depends on the temperature at which the eggs were incubated. Alligator eggs kept below a certain temperature will produce females. Above that temperature they will produce males.

HATCHING

When the embryo in an egg is fully developed, it starts to move. In birds, a special hatching muscle at the back of the chick's neck starts to twitch. This twitching action drives the chick's head backward and forward against the inside of the eggshell. A special "egg tooth" growing from the chick's beak makes a small hole in the shell. This process is known as pipping.

The chick can now breathe fresh air using its lungs, and it rests in order to build up strength. A few hours after pipping, the chick starts to cut its way out of the shell using its egg tooth. The parents only help the chick in a very few species, for example, the ostrich.

Reptile eggs hatch in much the same way as bird eggs. The young reptile's egg tooth, which grows from the top of the snout, disappears soon after hatching.

INSIDE AN EGG

Take off a small area of the wide end of the shell of an egg, a tiny piece at a time. Can you see the air space? Then carefully crack the egg onto a plate. Can you see the parts that are labeled in the top picture of an egg on page 18? The egg can be cooked and eaten when you have finished.

Egg cup holds egg steady

Membrane

CARE OF YOUNG

In some bird species, such as ducks and pheasants, the chicks can feed themselves as soon as they have hatched. In most species, however, newly hatched chicks are too small to fend for themselves. They must be fed by the parents. Often, the chicks start by eating food that has already been partly digested by one of the parents. As the chicks grow, they change to solid food.

Among some bird species that lay a pair of eggs, only the first chick to hatch receives any care. The second chick is not fed at all and quickly dies. This is not the parents being cruel. The second egg is just a safeguard in case the first does not hatch out.

Most young reptiles receive no care from their parents. The crocodile is one exception. The female parent picks up the hatchlings in her mouth, and carries them from the nest to the nearest water.

△ The gaping mouths of young robins make sure they are noticed and encourage the parents to bring food.

Internal fertilization is most highly developed in mammals. In order to increase the chances of fertilization, sperm is placed inside the female body close to the ovaries. The fertilized eggs then develop inside the female body until they are miniature versions of the adult, and ready for live birth.

COURTSHIP

As with most animals, courtship among mammals is concerned with attracting a mate. It may also stimulate the female to produce eggs. In many animals, the process of producing eggs is largely controlled by chemicals in the female body. These chemicals are hormones (substances that control body functions). In mammals the series of events involved in the production of eggs is known as the estrous cycle, and the time when eggs are produced as estrus. (Primates, including monkeys and humans, go through a rather similar cycle called the menstrual cycle.) In most mammals, estrus takes place regularly through the year. However, some mammals (again like many other animals) have breeding seasons at particular times of year, when courtship and mating take place.

If each female of a group mates with the strongest and healthiest of the available males, it helps to ensure that strong and healthy offspring are produced. For this reason, courtship among mammals sometimes consists of contests between competing males. These contests are simply symbolic in some species; for example, gazelles perform "dances." In other species, however, the contest involves fighting. The winner gains the prize of mating. The loser may even be killed, although this is very rare and only ever happens in a few species.

▷ Competing male giraffes fight by swinging their heads and necks at each other.

NESTS

Building nests is not essential in the reproduction of mammals because there is no need to incubate eggs. Some mammals do make a nest of some sort to protect the young and keep them warm. But whether they do depends largely on the overall characteristics of the species.

Many small mammals, such as mice, rabbits and foxes, live in burrows. This is where their young are born. Among larger mammals, the situation is more varied. Some species, such as horses and antelopes, make no preparations for birth. Their young are born out in the open. With other species, such as lions and tigers, the female will seek out a secure and sheltered place where the young can be born in safety.

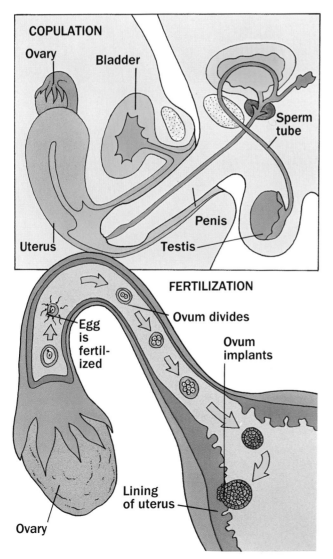

△ Fox cubs are born underground in safety. Only when they are more able to look after themselves do they emerge.

COPULATION

In mammals, fertilization is achieved by the act of copulation. During copulation, the male penis is placed inside the female vagina. Sperm are transferred to the female by the process of ejaculation. Sperm from the testes passes down the sperm tube and along the penis to the top of the vagina.

Each ejaculation transfers millions of sperm cells. These travel up through the uterus (or womb) toward the ovary. Fertilization occurs some time after copulation has taken place, when one sperm penetrates an egg just outside the ovary. The fertilized egg then passes down into the uterus. When the egg comes into contact with the lining of the uterus, it becomes attached to the surface and continues to develop.

Fertilization can only take place after the release of eggs (ova) by the ovaries — a process known as ovulation. In mammals with an estrous cycle, the female may release several eggs during estrus. There are some variations, for example, rabbits only ovulate after copulation. Primates, which have menstrual cycles, ovulate regularly about once every month. Any eggs that are not fertilized break up inside the uterus.

The number of eggs produced at each ovulation varies between different species. Most mammals produce more than one egg. They give birth to a number of offspring, each developed from a separate egg. Some larger mammals, such as horses and humans, normally produce just one egg at a time.

◁ Copulation leaves sperm at the top of the vagina. Sperm travel toward the ovary. One of the sperm fertilizes the egg. The fertilized egg, or zygote, travels toward the uterus. The zygote develops into a ball of cells before implanting in the lining of the uterus.

GESTATION

The development of a new mammal in its mother's uterus is known as gestation (or pregnancy). The length of gestation varies from one species to another. The longest gestation period is that of the Indian elephant at 22 months, while that of the hamster is only 16 days. In humans it is nine months.

In most mammals, the eggs become implanted in the uterus wall about four or five days after fertilization. The egg has by now developed into an embryo. A number of protecting membranes grow around the embryo. The innermost of these, the amnion, forms the amniotic sac. This is filled with fluid in which the embryo floats.

At first, the embryo is nourished by a small yolk sac. During the rest of its development, the embryo receives nourishment from the placenta. This develops from the lining of the uterus and is connected to the mother's blood supply. The embryo is joined to the placenta by the umbilical cord. While the embryo is developing, its blood travels along the cord to the placenta. In the placenta, nourishment and oxygen are absorbed into the embryo's blood and waste products are filtered out.

Quite early on in gestation, an embryo already has the beginnings of a head and four limbs. Then the embryo develops basic forms of all the organs and features that an adult has. This may be, for example, after about one quarter of gestation. From this point on, the new mammal is known as a fetus. At this stage, however, it is still too small and undeveloped to survive outside the parent. It stays inside the uterus until it is ready to be born.

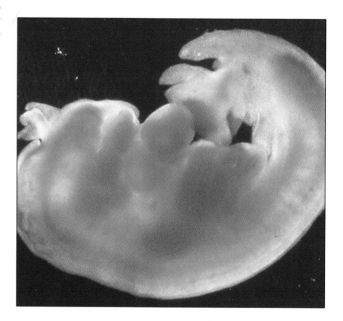

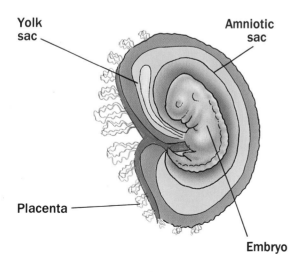

Yolk sac · Amniotic sac · Placenta · Embryo

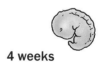

4 weeks

6 weeks

2 weeks

◁▷ Many monkeys have a gestation period of about 26 weeks. After two weeks the yolk supply is nearly used up. But the placenta is already well developed and connected to the embryo by the umbilical cord. Between the fourth and sixth weeks the embryo takes on a definite shape. By the tenth week most features have become visible. By the 18th week the young monkey is complete in most ways.

Mammals with long gestation periods, such as dolphins and apes, can only have about one pregnancy in a year. Species with short gestation periods, such as rats and mice, can have more than one pregnancy a year. The populations of such animals can increase very rapidly.

Some mammals, especially those that experience cold winters, have extended gestation periods. Badgers, for example, mate in July and August. Fertilized eggs develop normally for a few days, and move to the uterus. However, implantation does not take place, and the eggs stop developing. They remain in the uterus until January, when they implant, and continue their development. The young badgers are born in March.

MENSTRUAL CYCLE

Primates (including humans), which have a menstrual cycle, ovulate about once every month. Before each ovulation, the uterus prepares itself to receive a fertilized ovum (egg). This involves the surface layers of the uterus lining becoming thicker. An ovum is then released from an ovary. If the ovum is fertilized, it becomes implanted in the lining of the uterus. If it is not fertilized, after a few days the extra material of the uterus lining starts to break down. Then the ovum, material from the uterus and a certain amount of blood leave the body through the vagina. This is called menstruation.

◁▷ About a tenth of the way through gestation (left), the first features of the developing embryo appear. At this stage it is still difficult to see what anything will become. Halfway through gestation (right) most of the main features of the fetus are visible.

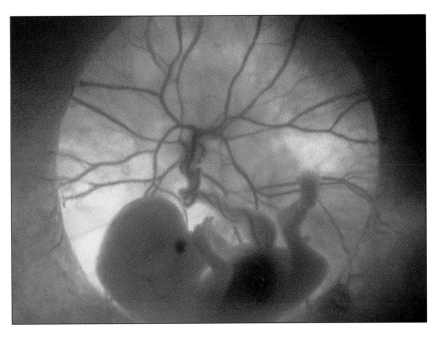

10 weeks

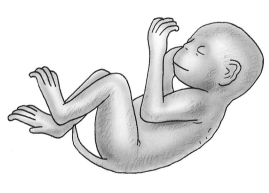

18 weeks

24 weeks

BIRTH

When a mammal fetus is fully developed, it is ready to be born. The birth process is divided into three stages. All stages involve powerful muscle movements in the body of the female parent. For this reason, the birth process is often known as "labor," especially when talking about humans.

During the first stage, the opening at the bottom of the uterus enlarges a great deal. The amniotic sac then bursts, releasing the fluid inside. The second stage is the birth itself. Muscle contractions force the offspring one at a time out of the female's body. As the young animals are forced out, the umbilical cords break, or else the mother bites them through. The new animal must now take its first breath. In the third stage, a final series of contractions forces out the placenta. At this time, the placenta is often called the afterbirth.

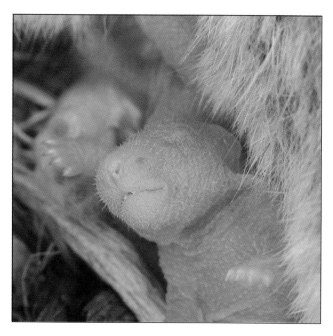

△ Newborn hamsters are blind, naked and helpless. Until their fur grows and their eyes open, they are entirely dependent on their mother.

DID YOU KNOW?

Like many young mammals, kittens are blind when they are born. Their eyes do not open for about two weeks. And when they do, kittens' eyes are always blue. Sometimes they stay blue, but in most breeds of cat a different eye color develops after a few weeks.

△ A newborn horse can stand up within minutes of birth, and can run about an hour later. In the wild, animals like the horse are hunted by predators. The young must be able to run away.

CARE OF YOUNG

As soon as a young mammal has been born, its mother usually licks it clean. The movement of the mother's tongue helps to clear out air passages (such as the nose) and may encourage the young animal to start breathing.

After a mammal has been born, it is no longer connected to its mother by the umbilical cord. But it still depends on its mother for food. All young mammals start feeding on milk, whatever they will eat as adults. The milk is made by special glands called mammary glands. It can be sucked from two or more nipples on the mother. Instinct makes newly born mammals suck at any nipple-shaped object.

In some species, such as deer and horses, the young can walk within an hour of birth. Such young animals need little care other than feeding. In other species, the young are helpless for some time, and need warmth and constant attention as well as food. This care is nearly always provided by the female parent. The mothers of most mammals will guard their offspring from danger.

△ As in all mammals, young orangutans feed on milk.

△ Female lions help to look after each other's cubs.

VIVIPAROUS ANIMALS

Not all insects, fish and reptiles lay eggs. Some are viviparous — they give birth to live young.

The female tsetse fly, for example, produces only one egg which she keeps in her body. The egg hatches, and the larva develops inside the female. The larva is not "born" until just before it takes on its adult form.

In fish, live birth is most common in sharks. The hammerhead shark, for instance, has a system for feeding an embryo that is quite similar to a mammal's placenta.

A type of live birth is fairly common among reptiles. Viviparous snakes and lizards usually live in colder climates where there is not enough warmth to incubate their eggs. Instead, the eggs are kept inside the female while the embryos develop. The eggs are laid only at the moment when they hatch.

△ The adder is one of the species of viviparous snake that live in colder climates.

THE SEAHORSE

Seahorses are among the most strangely shaped of all fish. They also have one of the most unusual forms of parenthood.

Male seahorses have a pouch with a spongy lining. It is on the front of the animal, near to the tail. During mating, a female seahorse lays her eggs directly into a male's pouch. The eggs become embedded in the spongy lining. While the eggs incubate, the lining provides them with oxygen. It also produces a nourishing fluid.

After the young seahorses have hatched, they remain inside the male's pouch until they are large enough to look after themselves. When they leave the pouch, it looks as if the male seahorse is giving birth to live young. During their first days of independent life, newly "born" seahorses sometimes hold onto the male with their tails.

△ A male seahorse's pouch can be clearly seen.

MONOTREMES

The monotremes are a group of egg-laying mammals. They are found only in Australasia. There are only three species: the duckbilled platypus, and two species of echidna (spiny anteater). Like birds, monotremes have only a single opening in their lower bodies — hence their name, which means "single outlet."

After mating and fertilization, a female monotreme lays one or two eggs. She incubates these with the warmth of her body. After the young hatch, they are fed on milk like other young mammals. Monotremes do not have nipples, however. Milk from the mammary glands just oozes to the surface.

△ The duckbilled platypus is a mammal that lays eggs.

MARSUPIALS

The marsupials are a large group of mammals with many different species. They are found only in Australasia (where most live) and the Americas. The embryo of a marsupial develops inside the female. But there is no placenta to provide it with food.

Marsupial embryos do not develop very far while still inside the female. They are very small when they are born. A kangaroo, for example, is only 0.5 inch long at birth. In some species, the lower half of the animal is completely unformed — the back legs are little more than bumps. The front legs, however, are well developed and equipped with claws. These claws are essential because the newborn offspring must climb up the female's body into a pouch of skin that surrounds the female nipples. Inside the pouch, marsupials continue to develop. They feed off milk from the nipples.

◁△ A newborn kangaroo may be holding on to one nipple in the pouch while an older kangaroo feeds from another. Young kangaroos that can hop still return to the pouch.

Every living cell contains coded information, known as genetic information. This information describes not only how each individual cell will develop, but also how a whole animal will develop. In animals that use sexual reproduction, the cells of the offspring have genetic information from both parents.

GENES AND CHROMOSOMES

Genetic information is carried by DNA (deoxyribonucleic acid). DNA is an extremely long molecule. It consists of a chain of many pairs of much smaller molecules (there are four types). The order of these pairs makes up the code for information. The chain can be divided into sections called genes. Each gene has the information for the development of one particular characteristic, such as the color of an animal's eyes.

DNA consists of two entwined helixes. The helixes are joined by the pairs of molecules. So DNA is rather like a twisted ladder. This double helix is, in turn, twisted around itself again and again. A huge amount of DNA twisted together can make up a chromosome.

Normally, DNA is spread out through the nucleus of a cell. When cell division is about to take place, the DNA arranges itself into chromosomes. This is so that mitosis or meiosis can take place (these are described on page 11).

The chromosomes in a cell are divided into pairs. Each pair has genes for the characteristics of the same things (for example, the color of the eyes). But these characteristics may be different (for example, brown eyes or blue eyes). To get more variety in the offspring, pairs of chromosomes exchange some genes in the first stage of meiosis.

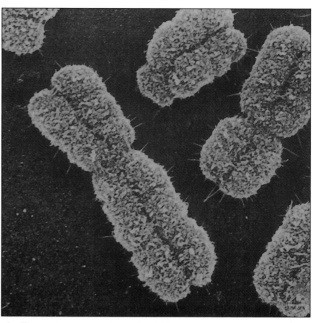

△ The chromosomes in this picture are divided into chromatids, joined at their middles. Each chromatid has exactly the same information. The Y-shaped chromosome is one that carries information for a mammal to be male.

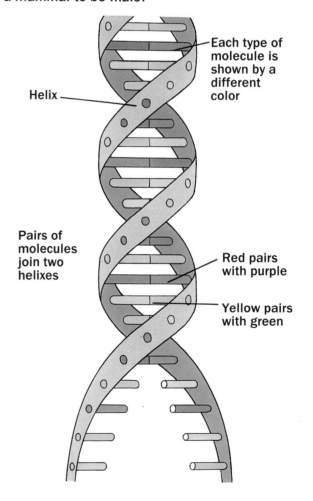

▷ The two halves of a DNA molecule can come apart like a zipper. A new half can "grow" on each original half. This produces two exact copies.

Helix

Each type of molecule is shown by a different color

Pairs of molecules join two helixes

Red pairs with purple

Yellow pairs with green

HEREDITY

Most of an animal's genes control the internal organization and working of its body. Most of these genes are the same in all healthy members of a species. Some genes, however, control characteristics that differ between individuals. These can vary because the differences do not significantly affect the health of the animal. Examples of such characteristics are the color of human eyes and the pattern of markings on a leopard's back. The transfer of characteristics from parents to their offspring is called heredity.

Some of the genes that control a particular characteristic have a stronger influence than others. The stronger genes are known as dominant. The weaker genes are called recessive. Understand-ing heredity involves understanding how genes operate in pairs.

The gene for a particular characteristic, such as the color of fur in cats, is located on both chromosomes of a pair. In a zygote, one half of each pair comes from each parent. If one parent has cont-ributed a dominant black-fur gene, and the other has contributed a recessive white-fur gene, the dominant gene will control development. The zygote will develop into a black cat.

The recessive white-fur gene may be passed on to this black cat's own off-spring. If both parents of a cat pass on this gene, the result is a white cat.

▽ This shows what might happen with two generations of cats. The gray gene is dominant and the orange recessive. Compare the colors of the cats to their genes.

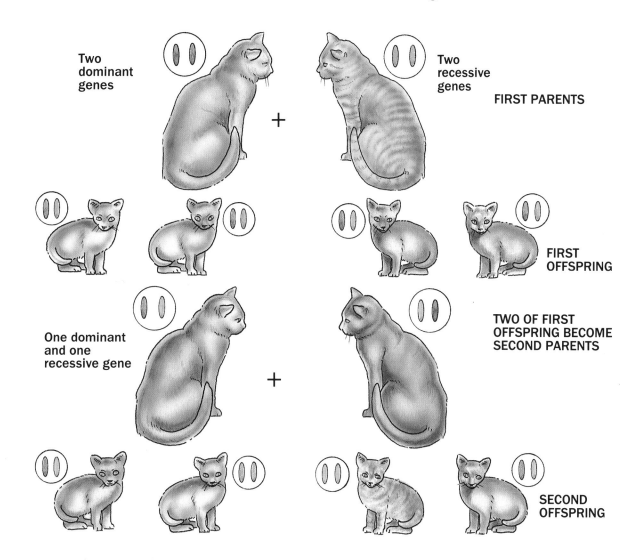

Two dominant genes

Two recessive genes

FIRST PARENTS

+

FIRST OFFSPRING

One dominant and one recessive gene

TWO OF FIRST OFFSPRING BECOME SECOND PARENTS

+

SECOND OFFSPRING

The scientific study of heredity began at the end of the last century. But it was not until the 1950s that scientists started to understand how DNA works. Since then, scientists have uncovered many of DNA's secrets. As a result, they have been able to manipulate genes and develop new techniques involving animal reproduction. These techniques are known as genetic engineering.

Cloning is a method of producing identical copies, called clones, of an animal or plant. Cloning occurs naturally in species that can reproduce by asexual methods. In other species, clones can be created in the laboratory. A clone can be made by replacing the nucleus of an egg cell with a nucleus from another cell. In theory, the new nucleus can be taken from a cell in any part of the body, or from a different animal if it belongs to the same species. The egg will then develop in the normal way into an exact duplicate of the animal from which the new nucleus was taken.

Cloning is still an experimental technique, and it is mainly carried out on small, simple animals. However, some larger animals have also been cloned. The first clones of an amphibian (a salamander) were produced in the 1950s, and the first mammals (mice) were cloned in 1981.

Other genetic engineering techniques involve making alterations to DNA itself. A section of DNA that contains a particular gene is cut out using special chemicals. The section is replaced by another section of DNA with a different gene. In this way, scientists can control the characteristics of a species.

Eventually, cloning and the alteration of DNA could produce animals or plants that are specially made for a particular purpose. For example, an animal could be given genes for characteristics that make it resistant to disease. At present, however, some people object to genetic engineering. They believe that it is dangerous and wrong to interfere with nature at such a basic level.

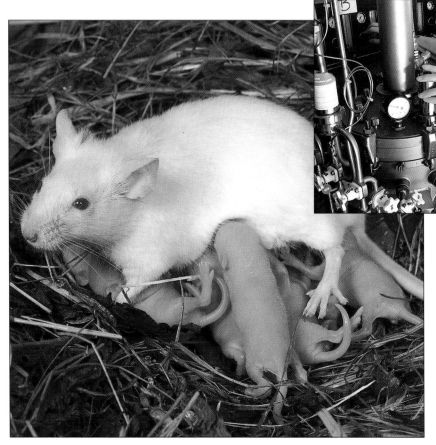

△ Genetic engineering is sometimes used in the production of medicines. The medicines are made by bacteria that have specially altered DNA.

◁ Mice were the first mammals to be successfully cloned. In theory, any animal can be cloned. Genetic engineering on humans is forbidden in most countries.

GLOSSARY

31

asexual
Without sex. The term is normally used to describe methods of reproduction that involve only one parent, called asexual reproduction.

chromosome
One of a pair of rods into which DNA arranges itself in a dividing cell.

copulation
The physical union between female and male animals that involves the transfer of sperm from the male to the female, and which allows internal fertilization to take place.

egg
A female sex cell produced by the ovaries; also called an ovum.

embryo
An animal during the early stages of development before hatching or birth.

fertilization
The process by which a female gamete (egg, or ovum) and male gamete (sperm) join to form a single cell that will develop into a new plant or animal.

fetus
An unborn mammal during the later stages of development in the uterus (womb).

gamete
A sex cell: an egg (ovum) in a female and a sperm in a male. The joining of female and male gametes is the basis of sexual reproduction.

gene
A section of DNA that refers to one particular inheritable characteristic.

genetics
The study of heredity and DNA.

gestation
The development of a young animal in the uterus; also called pregnancy.

heredity
The process of inheritance, by which particular characteristics are passed on from parents to their offspring.

incubation
The keeping of eggs at the right temperature for them to develop.

nucleus
The central part of a cell that stores DNA and controls the cell.

ovary
The female organ that produces eggs (ova). Most animals have two ovaries.

placenta
An organ that develops in the uterus of a pregnant mammal and provides nourishment to the unborn offspring.

pregnancy
Another name for gestation.

sperm
The male sex cell (gamete), produced by the testis.

testis
The male organ that produces sperm. Most animals have two testes.

uterus
The organ inside female mammals in which the young develop before birth; also called the womb.

womb
Another name for the uterus.

zygote
A fertilized egg (ovum) which will develop into a new individual.

Photographic Credits:
Cover and pages 8 top, 9 both, 12 both, 13, 14 both, 16, 18 both, 19 both, 24 all, 26 both, 27 both and 30 left: Bruce Coleman; pages 5, 21 and 25 bottom: Planet Earth Pictures; pages 6, 7, 8 bottom, 10, 22, 23, 28 and 30 right: Science Photo Library; pages 15 and 20: Eric and David Hosking; pages 17 both and 25 top: Frank Lane Picture Agency.

PRINTED IN BELGIUM BY
proost
INTERNATIONAL BOOK PRODUCTION